# URANUS

## in Signs, Houses and Aspects
## The Astrology of Unexpectation

## Thomas Canfield

## ACS Publications

by Thomas Canfield

International Standard Number
978-1-934-976-46-6

Library of Congress Control Number
2016903922

First Printing 2016

Printed in the United States of America


Published by
ACS Publications

an imprint of

Starcrafts LLC
334-A Calef Highway
Epping, New Hampshire  03042

*www.astrocom.com*

⛢

This book is
dedicated to
**Simonne Murphy**
who always reminds
me to be Uranian

# Table of Contents

# URANUS

(The author wishes it to be known that the proper pronunciation for Uranus is "you're-on-us" and not "your-anus.")

## Unexpectation: (noun) Lack of Expectation, want of foresight

# Chapter I
# A Planet named George

Discoveries that change the perception of the world and the universe are not always found in an expected manner. Like the European discovery of America, the discovery of Uranus was inadvertent, misunderstood, and not the first discovery. Just as Leif Ericson beat Columbus by 500 years, the first Astronomer Royal, John Flamsteed, noticed Uranus in the year 1690, but listed it as a new star. The French Astronomer Pierre Lemonnier made observations over a 19 year period, from 1750 to 1769, but he did not consider it to be a planet.

On March 13, 1781, William Herschel in Bath, England observed Uranus through his telescope, but even he did not consider it to be a planet. When he announced his discovery, he stated that he had found a comet. Other astronomers who plotted the orbit of this body realized that it was not the orbit of a comet, but of a planet. By 1783, even William Herschel was convinced that he had found a new planet. The result of the find was a galvanizing influence to the growing scientific community, and astronomers began speculating that there were other distant planets in the solar system.

As a reward for his discovery, William Herschel was given an annual stipend of 200 pounds by King George III. Herschel was obliged to move his telescope to Windsor Castle so that the royal family could look through it. When it came time to name the new planet, Astronomer Royal Nevil Maskelyne insisted that Herschel should have the honor. Herschel dubbed the new planet "Georgium Sidus" or "George's planet" in honor of his patron King George III.

However, Herschel's attempt at boot-licking did not gain much approval outside of Great Britain. French astronomer Jerome Lalande said the planet should be named "Herschel" after its discoverer. Swedish astronomer Erik Prosperin thought that it should be named "Neptune" to commemorate the victories of the British Navy.

Yet, it was the German astronomer Johann Elert Bode who suggested it should be named "Uranus", pointing out that as Saturn was the father of Jupiter, this new planet should be named for the father of Saturn. Bode's name was not immediately adopted, and it took more than 60 years before astronomers accepted it for universal usage. The British Nautical Almanac Office actually used "Georgium Sidus" until the year 1850.

As for a symbol for the new planet, French astronomer Lalande suggested a globe surmounted by the letter "H" for Herschel.

Other astronomers combined the symbols for the Sun and Mars, saying that was appropriate since Uranus was the god of the sky. For more than 200 years, the Sun-Mars symbol was mainly used in Europe. However, recently the H-globe symbol has been gaining in dominance.

Over the past two centuries, many discoveries have been made regarding Uranus which have marked it as the most unusual planet in the solar system. As early as 1789, William Herschel theorized that there might be Saturn-like rings around the planet. It was not until 1977 that astronomers James Eliot and Douglas Mink found that there really were rings around Uranus.

Their discovery was made by accident. Using the Kuiper Airborne Observatory, they were photographing Uranus at the time it "occulted," meaning passed in front of a star. When the pictures were developed, they found that the star was occulted five times before the planet passed in front of it. The presence of five rings around Uranus was proven by these pictures. Further rings were discovered by the Voyager 2 spacecraft and the Hubble Space Telescope.

In 1787, William Herschel discovered two moons orbiting around Uranus. He named them Titania and Oberon, after the royal fairies in Shakespeare's comedy, *A Midsummer Nights Dream.*

In 1851, two more moons of Uranus were discovered by William Lassell, and in 1948 Gerard Kuiper discovered a fifth large moon.

The first discovered five moons of Uranus have such mass that if they were orbiting the Sun on their own, they would be considered to be among the group of planets that are currently (as of 2006) defined by astronomers as "dwarf" or "minor" planets, or more recently the preferred term is said to be "small Solar System body." This group includes Ceres, Pluto, Eris, Makemake and Haumea.

The Voyager 2 space probe discovered 10 more moons of Uranus in 1986, and ground based telescopes discovered another nine moons by 1997. As moons are discovered, they are given the names of characters from Shakespeare, thereby continuing Herschel's tradition.

2

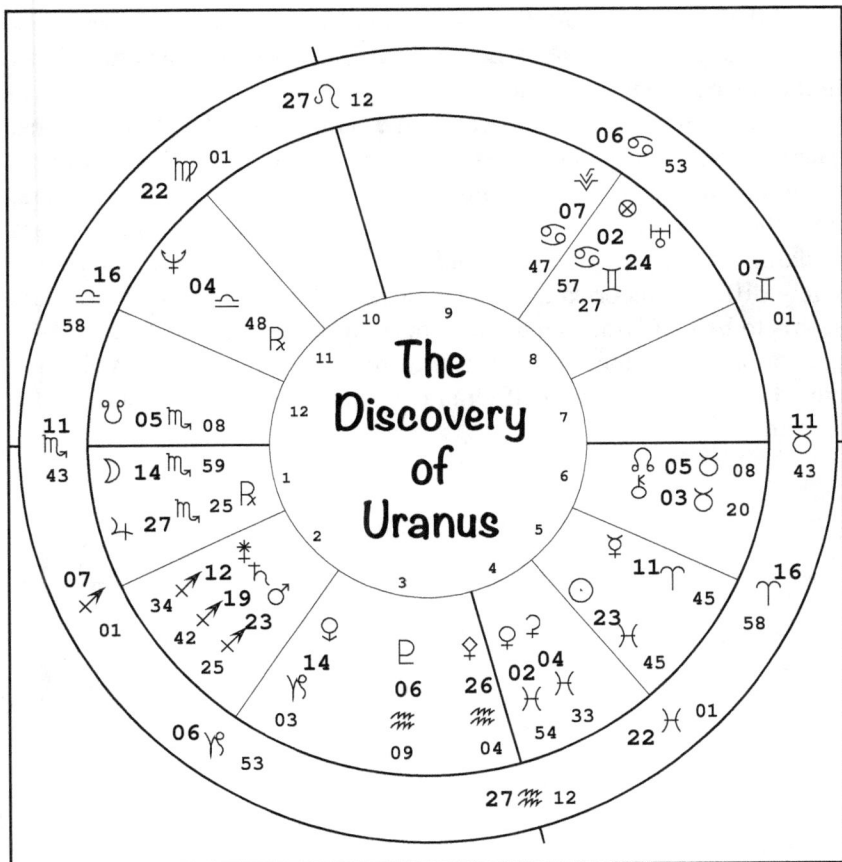

The Discovery of Uranus

The chart shown above is set for the exact moment and the exact location of William Herschel's first observation of Uranus through his telescope. The date, time and location at the time of his discovery was as follows:

### March 13, 1781
### 22h 39m LMT
### Bath, UK

Of course, this chart shows planets discovered since then, and the four major asteroids. It's interesting, though, to omit them, and see quite clearly, then, how Uranus closely squares Sun and opposes Mars, showing new and exciting work to come of this discovery!

3

Perhaps the oddest discovery about Uranus concerns its rotation. Uranus has an axis tilt of 98 degrees, which means it is the only planet in the solar system that rotates on its side.

In its 84 year journey around the Sun, Uranus has four seasons, each of which lasts about 21 years. A person standing on the North Pole of Uranus would see the Sun moving in a widening circle for 21 years, until the Sun went below the horizon, and then there would be 42 years of darkness until the Sun appeared above the equator. There have been a few different theories about this unusual axis. The most prominent seems to be that Uranus may have been hit by a larger body during its primordial formation, causing its axis to be radically tilted. With each new discovery, it seems as if Uranus is the weirdest planet in the solar system.

# Chapter 2

# The British Angels Fight Over Uranus

So, how did astrologers take to the new planet? It seems they did not warm up to it at once. Ebenezer Sibley mentioned "Herschel" in a few of his articles, but he offered no interpretation nor suggested what sign it ruled. That task was not undertaken until the year 1828, when John Varley, an astrologer and friend of William Blake, published *A Treatise on Zodiacal Physiognimy*, in which he stated that Uranus was the ruler of Aquarius.

Varley decided that Uranus ruled sudden and violent change, after an experience with his horoscope in which Uranus was in an "evil aspect" just as Varley's house burned down. No one has found any earlier record of Uranus being associated with Aquarius.

Enter, then, the British Angels, three prominent almanac publishers named Raphael, Zadkiel, and Sepharial. It was Raphael who took up the cause of Uranus as ruler of Aquarius, and made tentative statements that the new planet deserved to supplant Saturn as the ruler of Aquarius. However, Zadkiel responded with a statement that Raphael's assignment of Uranus to rule Aquarius was hasty, and that more research needed to be done in the matter. Sepharial entered the fray by writing that Uranus should not be assigned to any zodiacal sign, but conceded that it did belong in the Air triplicity.

By the 20th century, the status of Uranus was still up in the air, and the noted astrological author Alan Leo admitted in 1909 that Uranus had not been given a zodiacal rulership, though Aquarius had been suggested.

Then, as astrology gained more of a following within the new century, more astrological authors, most notably Evangeline Adams, began to accept Uranus as the ruler of Aquarius. What had started out as a tentative suggestion then became a standard notion, probably because no one else could suggest an alternate sign.

Metaphysical astrologers came to see Uranus as a higher octave of Mercury. If Mercury ruled communication, writing, and books for an individual chart, then Uranus was seen to rule mass communication, electronic writing, and instant transmission of information.

Also, Uranus had been discovered at a time when three great revolutions coincided: the American Revolution, the French Revolution, and the Industrial Revolution. So the spirit or Uranus could be seen in the mass movements and upheavals that were caused by these revolutions in which old orders were overthrown and new patterns of thinking were spread around the world.

The American Revolution was fought when Uranus was in Gemini, and revoltionary publications prompted the separation from Great Britain. The most revolutionary pamphlet of 1776 was Thomas Paine's *Common Sense*, which outlined the reasons why America should be a separate and independent nation from Great Britain. The spirit of the revolution was to be found in Thomas Jefferson's writing of *The Declaration of Independence*. It was a war that would be fought with public opinion and newspapers, as well as on the battlefield. The result was that documents from the revolutionary period would take on the role of political scripture, used to guide the legal developments of future generations.

The French Revolution began with Uranus in Leo, and the undoing of centralized power which had been the goal of Louis XIV, the Sun King. Control of the nation of France shifted from Versailles to the revolutionary councils that demanded more power until nobles and members of the royal family were offered up as blood sacrifices. The revolutionary fervor would climax in what Robespierre called his "cult of reason", but which historians have dubbed "the reign of terror." By the time Uranus moved into Virgo, the French Revolution had settled down to the more bourgeois leadership of the Directory, with Napoleon Bonaparte waiting in the wings.

The Industrial Revolution began in the 1760's, with Uranus in Aries marking development of the steam engine, leading to the creation of steamships and railroads, bringing different groups together by faster means, actually improving the gene pool of nations. It marked an attitude change that machines might be able to do things better than people or animals, prompting further mechanical developments through the 19th century.

# Chapter 3
# The Mythology of Uranus

Uranus has the distinction of being the only planet named for a Greek deity of classical mythology. All the other planets were given the Roman names of the gods. In Greek mythology, Uranus was the god of the sky, supposedly created out of primordial chaos. There was no cult of Uranus that survived until the period of recorded history. In that sense, Uranus was a long-neglected deity, almost as obscure as the planet was.

In the Greek creation mythology, the sky-god Uranus would cover the Earth each night, and mate with the Earth goddess, Gaia. In an age before birth control, poor Gaia was forced to give birth to giants. Her first dozen children were known as the Titans. Then she gave birth to three one-hundred armed giants known as Hekatonkheires, and finally she gave birth to three one-eyed giants known as the Cyclops. Uranus was not exactly a nurturing father, and he ended up imprisoning his offspring in the underground regions of Tartarus. The imprisonment of her children (and the constant child-bearing) gave great pain to Gaia. She begged her children to overthrow their father, and only the Titan Kronos (aka Saturn) was willing to take the risk.

According to one account, Kronos castrated Uranus as he was about to impregnate Gaia again. According to another account, the other Titans held down Uranus as Kronos castrated him. From that time on, the sky and the Earth were completely separate, and Uranus would keep his distance from Gaia. Some versions of the story said that the blood of Uranus spawned races of monsters like the nymphs and the furies. The testicles of Uranus supposedly fell into the ocean and brought about the creation of Aphrodite, goddess of love.

7

The continuing story of Greek mythology had Kronos locking up his brothers in Tartarus, and then taking his sister, Rhea, as his wife. It was Rhea who was the mother of the classical deities: Hades, Hestia, Hera, Poseidon, Demeter, and Zeus. Uranus predicted that a child of Kronos would overcome the castrating Titan. So, Kronos swallowed up his children as soon as they were born, except for Zeus who was hidden away by Rhea. When Zeus was fully grown, he fulfilled the prophecy of overcoming Kronos by getting the Titan to vomit up all the other children. Zeus also released the giants in Tartarus to join in the fight against Kronos, who was later imprisoned in Tartarus.

While the Greek pantheon brought about major changes on Earth, Uranus was left alone and neglected. Because of the negative end to the mythology, some astrologers have questioned whether Uranus is the correct name for a planet that rules revolutions. A few have suggested the planet should be renamed "Prometheus" after the Titan who gave fire to humanity. Yet, in considering revolutions, one should realize that they usually end up producing their own "Titans" who invariably fight among themselves, with some as winners and others coming out as the losers.

Uranus may be seen as the progenitor of revolutions, but there is no guarantee of a successful outcome. While one revolution may produce a Washington, another revolution may produce a Napoleon.

Revolutions also reach a point where castration enters in and the leadership gets cut down, bringing in a new leadership with a more somber or "saturnine" approach. In France, the violent leadership of Robespierre gave way to the more pragmatic leadership of Barras and the Directory. In the Industrial Revolution, steam engines came under the control of corporations who built the steam ships and set the directions for the railroads. Even in America, the leadership of Washington was undone by the constant stabbings of partisan newspapers, forcing him to reach the conclusion that two terms were enough for any president. So, with Uranus, change happens, and then it settles down to business as usual.

The occultist Aleister Crowley suggested that Pan was an incarnation of Uranus, since Pan was the god of music and science. Pan also had wild episodes, from which we derive the word "panic." Crowley regarded Uranus as the planet of magical power, Kundalini energy, and the illumination of genius, which can often be mistaken for madness. In Crowley's case, with Uranus in opposition to Saturn, there were many who assumed he was a madman since he broke down old manners and morals with his unconventional views. As a result, he had a fine understanding of Uranus as the planet of "the Magician."

# Chapter 4
# Uranus through the Zodiac
# A Historical Overview

As one of the outer planets, Uranus tends to mark people in a generational manner. Its meaning can stand for the changes that take place between one generation and another. Uranus takes seven years to go through each sign, and completes an orbit of the Sun in about 84 years. Examining the seven year cycles in the path of history can show certain trends that can be attributed to the planetary symbolism. The first paragraph in each sign is a general interpretaition of Uranus in that sign. The following paragraph(s) describe historical events of the period.

## Uranus in Aries

In Aries, Uranus represents a drive for freedom and independence. Unconventional ideas and a willingness to follow a unique leader can be seen during these years. An interest in machinery, electronics, and new technology will be found here. Pioneering spirits and impulsive behavior may both be seen. It might seem at times that some people are lacking tact and self-control, but they may be responding to the abrupt and radical changes taking place.

**From 1760 to 1768, Uranus was in Aries at the time James Watt was developing the steam engine, the major source of travel power into the 19th century.** There had been steam engine experiments before, but Watt was the one who came up with a practical design, which would power railroads and ships. It was also at this time that France lost her American colonies, and friction began to develop between Great Britain and the British colonies in America. "No taxation without representation" became the rallying cry leading up to the American Revolution. This transit saw the births of some innovative geniuses, such as Robert Fulton (developer of the steamship), Eli Whitney (inventor of the cotton gin), and Benjamin Latrobe (architect of the U.S. Capitol and other Federal buildings.)

**Uranus returned to Aries from 1844 to 1851, just in time for Samuel Morse's invention of the telegraph, which introduced the era of electronic communication.** "What hath God wrought" was the first electronic message sent. (The second was a greeting from former first lady Dolley Madison to a friend in Baltimore.)

In Europe, revolutions broke out in France, Austria, and Hungary, prompting Karl Marx to write "The Communist Manifesto." Gold was discovered in California, starting a major migration to the West Coast. Born under this transit were some of the greatest inventor-businessmen of the 19th century; Thomas Edison, George Westinghouse, and Alexander Graham Bell.

**Electronic communication made advancement when Uranus was in Aries from 1927 to 1935.** The coming of Talkies shook up the motion picture industry and removed dozens of silent film stars who had poor voices. The radio industry became regulated and began expanding, starting with 16 radio stations forming the Columbia Broadcasting System. It was a time when charismatic leaders took advantage of the new media formats to rise to power. Stalin in Russia, Hitler in Germany, and Franklin Roosevelt in America all made frequent use of newsreels and radio. This transit brought forth the space race generation in the 1960's, particularly the Apollo 11 astronauts, Neil Armstrong, Buzz Aldrin, and Michael Collins.

**Since March, 2011, Uranus has been in Aries, and will be there until March, 2019.** So far, this period has shown an increase in advanced electronics, as demonstrated by the proliferation of Smart Phones. (The current joke is a Smart Phone is outdated as soon as you take it out of the box.) New advancements in wind power, solar power, and even fracking may supply the energy sources that are needed to power all our electronic toys.

In the world of politics, there is a constant debate about government control, especially over firearms and military assault weapons being owned by citizens. Another debate issue is the subject of drones and the ethics of using controlled machines to kill in a war zone. At present, it is too early to say what sort of geniuses will be born under this transit. However, Beyonce Knowles has announced that her daughter, Blue Ivy, was able to read flash cards at age one. An indication of genius to come?

# Uranus in Taurus

There may be a sense of rebellion against authority, causing authority to crack down even more, thereby causing more rebellion. Economic problems may appear, with certain persons worrying about a major loss. People will start thinking of alternatives, and there may be planning for major changes. Individuals will join together to struggle for a greater cause, even if the cause they are fighting for seems futile against overwhelming oppression.

**From 1768 to 1775, the big issue in Great Britain and America was taxation.** Great Britain felt that Americans should be supporting the empire. Americans were willing to do their share, but were against tax rates imposed upon them by Parliament. As protest, the Americans began a boycott of British goods. Most notably, tea was boycotted because of the tax upon it, even though the colonials paid a lesser tax than the average Englishman. The increased agitation against tea brought about destruction of property in the Boston Tea Party, resulting in punitive measures taken against the city of Boston.

British repression was at its highest as Uranus was about to leave Taurus. Under this transit, the world witnessed the births of domineering and dynamic figures such as Napoleon Bonaparte, the Duke of Wellington, and Ludwig van Beethoven.

**Uranus came back to Taurus from 1851 to 1858, a period of further agitation in the United States over two issues, immigration and slavery.** Violent arguments against immigration and hatred towards Roman Catholics brought about the rise of the "Know Nothing" Party, one of those single-issue political groups which had brief control.

Northern states began increased agitation against slavery in the Southern states, prompted by the Fugitive Slave Law, the compelling novel "Uncle Tom's Cabin", and the Dred Scott decision by the Supreme Court, which said a black man had no rights a white man was bound to respect. This decision wiped away all compromises between North and South, and established the slave power as being protected by the Constitution. This transit saw the births of nation-building figures such as Emperor Mutsuhito of Japan, Cecil Rhodes, and Woodrow Wilson

**The next transit of Uranus into Taurus from 1935 to 1942** saw the rise of fascist domination in Europe. Mussolini's armies conquered Ethiopia. Germany and Italy teamed up to aid General Franco in Spain against the Republican government. Hitler managed to get bloodless conquests in the Rhineland, Austria, and Czechoslovakia. Then he

11

turned to violent means to expand his empire into Poland, Denmark, Norway, France, and Russia.

By the time Uranus was ready to leave Taurus, the domination of the Axis powers was at its high water mark. Some politically controlling figures born at this time were Saddam Hussein, Dick Cheney, and John Dean.

# Uranus in Gemini

This is a time of rebellion again tyranny, with liberation and new ideals for the masses. The literature of freedom is enhanced with the writings of visionaries who inspire the people with high ideals. Old structures will not stand against the tide of revolutionary thought. Personal relationships could be disrupted and family ties broken in the fight for the greater good. It is a time out of the ordinary, likely to be the subject of novels and major motion pictures.

**Uranus was in Gemini during the American Revolution from 1775 to 1782, and this conflict brought literary genius to the forefront in the struggle against Great Britain**. America's most prominent publisher, Benjamin Franklin, was sent as a diplomat to France, where he was able to arrange an alliance with King Louis XVI against King George III. With the help of France, George Washington was able to defeat the British at Yorktown in 1781, ending the struggle.

Uranus in Gemini also saw the birth of "The Great Triumvirate", three Senators who would stir the 19th century with their rhetoric; Henry Clay, John C. Calhoun, and Daniel Webster.

**From 1858 to 1866, Uranus in Gemini marked the Civil War, and the first Uranus return in the chart of the USA**. What began as a war to preserve the Union, quickly became a crusade against slavery, with the Emancipation Proclamation (and later the 13th Amendment) removing the scourge that had afflicted the American body politic. Generations of Abolitionists were vindicated as their work came to fruition after decades of writing books, articles, and sermons against slavery. The Civil War was the first modern war to be chronicled with telegraph reports, photographs and woodcut illustrations, which were printed in publications with wide circulation. Born at this time were high-minded reformers like William Jennings Bryan, Theodore Roosevelt, and William Randolph Hearst.

**During World War II, the Axis tide of power began to decline once Uranus entered Gemini, and from 1942 to 1949 the powers of**

**the world focused on the extermination of the fascism that had risen up in the 1930's.** The United Nations created a new ideal for world peace and cooperation between nations. Internationalism triumphed over isolationism as politicians realized they could not hide from the changes in the world. The expansion of Communism brought about a Cold War that lasted for generations, but there were still positive ideals to be praised, such as the Marshall Plan to rebuild Europe after the war. Future leaders such as Bill Clinton, George W. Bush, and Dan Quayle were born under this transit.

# Uranus in Cancer

This could be a period of touchy feelings and hypersensitivity, which can make the public aware of the problems at hand, but without providing any solutions. People may start thinking about "the good old days" and resent new ideas and changes. There might be a public reaction against new policies, but in the end the forces of reaction will be swept away. People are likely to be swayed by emotional appeals rather than the force of reason. A strong leader, such as a military man, might provide a father figure to the masses and win their support through appeals to patriotism.

**From 1782 to 1788, while Uranus was in Cancer, the United States was ruled by the Articles of Confederation, which gave all the authority to the states.** The Congress of the Confederation was a powerless entity, which could not pass any national laws unless all states agreed. (Since the state of Rhode Island refused to send a delegation, almost no laws were passed.)

The trend towards anarchy was underscored by Shay's Rebellion, a mini-civil war in Massachusetts. This prompted a call for a stronger national government, which resulted in the Constitutional Convention in 1787, presided over by George Washington.

The cause of the new Constitution was promoted by Alexander Hamilton, James Madison, and John Jay in "The Federalist Papers", but it was the reputation of Washington that made people support the new government. Once the Constitution was ratified in 1788, the way was set for George Washington to become the first President of the United States. Born under this transit were future Presidents Martin Van Buren and Zachary Taylor, as well as the great naturalist John James Audubon.

**Uranus returned to Cancer from 1866 to 1872, during the period of Reconstruction and a rebuilding of the South after the Civil War.** At first, it looked like there was hope for civil rights and new prospects for the black population, but Southern whites formed the Ku Klux Klan to terrorize the former slaves into submission. The election of Ulysses S. Grant brought a period of stability, but the economy started to experience major changes.

Powerful corporations rose up and began influencing political movements. The power grab by corporations was best shown by the Tweed Ring in New York City, which authorized millions to be spent on civic improvements, only to have the money go to dummy corporations controlled by the politicians. It would not be until after Uranus left Cancer, that a period of reform began to clean out the crooks.

In Europe, the newly formed German Empire destroyed the French Empire under Napoleon III, and under the administration of Bismarck, Germany set out to be the dominant power on the continent with threats of militarism.

This transit of 1866-1872 also marked the births of powerful figures such as conductor Arturo Toscanini, architect Frank Lloyd Wright, and scientist Marie Curie.

**Uranus in Cancer from 1949 to 1956 brought a period of fear caused by the "Red Scare."** Communists were supposed to have infiltrated the government and were threatening to overthrow the American way of life. (In Russia, at the same time, there were fears that "capitalists" had corrupted the government officials, and they needed to be purged before they overthrew the system.)

The Communist takeover of China and the start of the Korean War increased the paranoia towards Communism, which was exploited by Senator Joseph McCarthy, who cast false accusations of Communist conspiracies to enhance his own reputation. Yet, by 1954, McCarthy had gone too far with his charges and was exposed as a charlatan.

The election of Dwight Eisenhower as President brought a calming influence, and his work in ending the Korean War and starting a policy of "Coexistence" with the Soviet Union did much to relieve tensions. People were able to relax and focus on the marvels of the age, such as television. At this time were born cerebral figures such as Steve Jobs, Steve Wozniak, and Andy Hertzfeld, who would influence the lives of millions by the end of the century.

# Uranus in Leo

Dramatic gestures and a revolutionary love for freedom characterize this transit. Headstrong behavior and forceful actions will be found here. It is a time for adventures, and not for being ordered around. Love relations may be eccentric, and there may be unusual attractions between individuals. There may be a sense of idealism, but the practical measures that are needed to carry out ideas may not be well-developed. Expansion and achievement are the goals to live by at this time

**The Uranus in Leo cycle from 1788 to 1795 was an intense period for France as the nation was wracked by revolution.** The monarchy was overthrown and a republic was established. However, the leaders of the republic could not agree on a practical policy. This brought about the "reign of terror" in which factions sent their political rivals to the guillotine. Stability was brought about by a new government called the Directory, which used the talents of a young general named Napoleon Bonaparte to restore order. France not only had to deal with disorder at home, but the nation had to fight a coalition of nations trying to restore the monarchy.

**In the United States, there was a political division leading to the formation of different parties.** Supporters of Jefferson and Madison wanted to give more assistance to France, while supporters of Washington and Hamilton wanted a more neutral approach by negotiation with Great Britain. This period also saw "the Whiskey Rebellion", an uprising by Pennsylvania farmers against the Whiskey Tax. Controversial leaders born at this time included Antonio Lopez de Santa Anna, John Tyler, and James Buchanan.

**The next Uranus in Leo cycle from 1872 to 1878 saw a period of technological advancement, best shown by the marvels at the Centennial Exhibition in 1876.** Alexander Graham Bell demonstrated his telephone there, and the endorsement of Brazilian Emperor Dom Pedro II helped the new invention to achieve national interest.

Edison had begun his laboratory work, resulting in the inventions of the stock ticker, the phonograph, and experiments in electricity leading up to the electric light. George Westinghouse set up a company to manufacture railroad air brakes and signals, and would later be involved in electrical work with Nikola Tesla. Andrew Carnegie recognized the value of steel for bridges and building construction, and set up the first modern steel factory in Pittsburgh. Among the luminaries born under this transit were D.W. Griffith, Albert Schweitzer, and Thomas Mann.

**Uranus in Leo from 1956 to 1962 saw the beginnings of the "Space Race", as the USA and the Soviet Union began competing with space launches.**

The Soviets started the race with the launching of Sputnik, which prodded the American space program to hurry up. There were also fears of a "missile gap" in which the Soviet Union would have more missiles to carry nuclear warheads. Science and space studies became featured parts of education. The Soviet Union would launch the first man into space, but the USA quickly caught up with the Project Mercury program.

**The climax of Uranus in Leo would be John Glenn's flight as the first American in space, with three orbits around the Earth.** Glenn would return to Earth as a hero, achieving national acclaim. Famous figures born under this transit were Barack Obama, Ellen Degeneres, and Michael Jackson.

# Uranus in Virgo

Things may seem quieter and more conservative, but beneath the surface there is still a rage against repression. There may be a need to investigate and find the true cause of problems. Yet, there is also a feeling that dramatic action is needed to solve these problems, even if some people may get hurt. Trouble behind the scenes may thwart serious goals, and a strong public gesture may be needed to make change happen. Complacency gives way to upheaval, and a new broom ends up sweeping clean.

**Uranus in Virgo from 1795 to 1801 marked the time of the Directory in France. Napoleon Bonaparte was kept busy invading Italy and later Egypt.** Foreign Minister Talleyrand tried to bring in extra income by demanding "gifts" from American diplomats. This insulting request for a bribe nearly resulted in a war between France and the United States. Americans responded with the cry of "Millions for defense, but not one cent for tribute", and a wave of Anti-French sentiment went over the land.

**The Alien and Sedition Acts were put into effect to deport unwanted immigrants and to arrest newspaper editors who insulted the government.** Ironically, there was sedition with Alexander Hamilton receiving reports from cabinet officers, essentially running a shadow government behind the back of President John Adams.

The relationship between France and the USA improved once Napoleon overthrew the Directory and set up his own Consular government. Among the famous born at this time were Horace Mann, Franz Schubert, and Alexander Pushkin.

**The Uranus in Virgo cycle from 1878 to 1885 saw the rise of Trusts, large corporate structures which brought about the control of wealth by a small group of men.** Labor was organizing to resist corporate domination. Out West, Native Americans struggled to keep their lands, but were eventually forced onto reservations. Civil rights for freed slaves were declared unconstitutional, removing many legal protections which had been attained after the Civil War. Against government oppression, new groups of Anarchists and Nihilists arose. Assassinations killed Czar Alexander II of Russia and President James Garfield. Important figures born were Albert Einstein, Margaret Sanger, and Ethel Barrymore.

**More assassinations would take place during the Uranus in Virgo cycle from 1962 to 1969.** John F. Kennedy, Martin Luther King Jr., and Robert Kennedy would be gunned down, and to this day conspiracy theories about their deaths still abound.

**Uranus conjunct Pluto in 1966 brought a period of cultural upheaval, as protests began against the Vietnam War, the repression of civil rights, and the stodgy morals of the older generation.** Free love, the drug culture, and rock music shocked the older generation and gave new perspectives for viewing the world. Among the love children born during these years were Johnny Depp, Dan Brown, and J.K. Rowling.

# Uranus in Libra

Artistic ability and diplomacy go wild as unexpected developments take place. Marriages and relationships may only be temporary as rapid new connections are made. Strong political structures or alliances may be shaken and broken as new events occur. Even the spirit of fame may seem transitory. Accomplishments may not last as surprise events change the nature of success.

**From 1801 to 1807 saw the further rise of Napoleon Bonaparte, from First Consul to Emperor and master of most of Europe.** Although he had a reputation as a conqueror, the beginning of his end would take place in 1807 at the battle of Eylau, which ruined his reputation as an infallible warrior. In America, President Thomas Jefferson gained fame with the negotiation of the Louisiana Purchase, and later with the war against the Barbary Pirates. However, his fame waned in his second administration, especially with an embarrassing treason trial against Aaron Burr, in which Jefferson had to invoke "executive privilege" in withholding certain evidence. Great explorations were made in the Louisiana Territory by Lewis and Clark. Charismatic figures born at this time were Robert E. Lee, Benito Juarez, and Joseph Smith.

**Uranus in Libra from 1885 to 1891 saw a period of economic expansion, and the growth of modern navies, in which steel battleships replaced wooden vessels.** A significant invention at the time was Kodak film on celluloid strips, making it easier for taking photographs, and eventually leading to the creation of moving pictures. Powerful artists like Paul Gauguin and Vincent Van Gogh produced their greatest works in this period. Other great talents born at this time were Al Jolson, Charles Chaplin, and Alexander Woollcott.

**From 1969 to 1975, diplomacy did the twist with Uranus in Libra.** The Vietnam War was brought to an end, but two years later the North Vietnamese would sweep away the treaty, sweep over South Vietnam, and sweep out the American presence. Staunch anti-Communist Richard Nixon went to China for a meeting with Chairman Mao Zedong, making his new connection with Red China a negotiating tool against the Soviet Union in arms talks. Nixon's fame for this diplomacy was undone by the Watergate scandal, and despite his efforts to invoke "executive privilege", evidence came out to indicate his guilt, bringing about his resignation. In motion pictures and magazines, explicit sexuality came to the forefront as old moral restrictions fell by the wayside. Sexy and talented performers such as Heather Graham, Uma Thurman, and Tina Fey were born at this time.

# Uranus in Scorpio

Determination and persistence can not be broken by resistance. A resolution to stand firm may lead to conflict, but it also may lead to greater respect. Economic difficulties may abound. Money problems for the masses may shake loyalties, but old structures may remain firm. Suspicions of covert activities may lead to investigations. The desire for self-advancement may take precedence over group activity.

**From 1807 to 1814, Uranus in Scorpio saw Napoleon Bonaparte's decline, first with an ill-advised invasion of Spain, and then with a worse invasion of Russia.** By 1813, a coalition of nations was forcing the French army back into their own country, resulting in the abdication of Napoleon and his exile to Elba. In America, President Jefferson, and then President Madison resisted the call to war by restricting trade with Europe. The Embargo Act created economic problems for New England, and was eventually overturned.

**By 1812, no further diplomacy was possible, and war with Great Britain was declared.** American attempts to invade Canada were met with resistance. British forces burned Washington D.C. in retaliation for burning York, Ontario. However, the British were repulsed at Baltimore, giving new fighting spirit and a new national anthem to the Americans. Prominent figures born under this transit were Charles Darwin, Abraham Lincoln, and Charles Dickens.

**Uranus in Scorpio from 1891 to 1898 saw a period of economic collapse, with gold reserves being drained out of the U.S. Treasury.** There was agitation against the Gold Standard, lead by William Jennings Bryan in his "Cross of Gold" speech. Trusts consolidated their power, and used military force against organized labor. Yet, working men continued to rally towards unions. Prosperity returned in 1898 with the Spanish-American war, and the United States gained new territory and resources, making it a global power. Important figures born under this transit were J.R.R. Tolkien, Mary Pickford, and Mao Zedong.

**Uranus in Scorpio included a period of economic upheaval that took place from 1975 to 1981** A recession with high inflation and unemployment was going on, stagnating financial growth. High interest rates were good for those keeping their savings in Certificates of Deposit and retirement accounts, but businesses found it difficult to get loans.

Right-wing movements, such as the Moral Majority began rising up, resulting in the election of Ronald Reagan. During this transit, the Soviet Union invaded Afghanistan, a move which has been considered to be the beginning of the end for the Soviet empire.

This was also a period of wilder sexual activity, especially among the Gay community. However, the discovery of the HIV virus and other sexually transmitted diseases put an end to promiscuous behavior. Attractive figures born at this time were Orlando Bloom, Ashton Kutcher, and Jennifer Love Hewitt.

# Uranus in Sagittarius

A visionary spirit or a sense of idealism may pervade individuals born under this transit. A love for science or travel to exotic places may be part of the personal potential. However, theoretical ideas of a better world may not always work out in practical reality. Unorthodox or risky ventures might be considered to further abstract visions of morality and a better world view. Anything produced under this transit may be focused on the betterment of humanity, and that may be the focus for broadening your point of view.

**"The Era of Good Feeling" was the name given to the period from 1814 to 1820 when Uranus was in Sagittarius.** The War of 1812 ended with the United States giving Great Britain a resounding defeat at the battle of New Orleans (which took place three weeks after the peace treaty was signed.) The Duke of Wellington put an end to Napoleon's plans for regaining power with a major victory at the Battle of Waterloo. Napoleon was sent off to St. Helena in exile for the rest of his life.

In England, Jane Austen's novels were capturing the ladies of Regency society. Rebellion was breaking out among the Latin American colonies of Spain, prompting the United States to take a greater role in the spread of freedom in the Western Hemisphere. As more states entered the Union, Henry Clay took the forefront in devising the Compromise of 1820, which established a 30-year balance between slave states and free states. Among the leaders born under this transit were Queen Victoria, Otto von Bismarck, and Baha'u'llah, founder of the Baha'i religion.

**Uranus returned to Sagittarius from 1898 to 1904, in a period where anarchists were rebelling against the established order.** The Empress of Austria, the King of Italy, and President McKinley were all shot by anarchists. McKinley's death brought Theodore Roosevelt to the Presidency, where he began reforms in regard to the nature of government power.

Previously, government power had been used to protect the interests of big business. Roosevelt turned government power against abuses of big business, starting a program of "trust busting" to break up corporations that had gotten too large. Roosevelt's reforms were so popular that he was the first Vice-President to become President and then be re-elected.

It was also under this Uranus in Sagittarius that Nikola Tesla began experiments in wireless telegraphy, but he was beaten in its development by Marconi's first radio transmissions. Also, a couple of bicycle repairmen from Dayton, OH named Orville and Wilbur Wright flew the first heavier-than-air flying machine, thereby proving wrong all the people who said, "If God meant man to fly, He would have given us wings."

Talented people born at this time included Ernest Hemingway, producer Irving Thalberg, and Ezra Taft Benson, future President of the Mormon church.

**The Roosevelt reforms seemed to come undone, though, during the next time Uranus was in Sagittarius, from 1981 to 1988.** These were the years of the "Reagan Revolution," when deregulation and a loosening of government control helped the world of big business. Government was declared to be the problem, not the solution.

This time also saw the rise of international terrorism, with suicide car bombings and kidnappings of important Americans in the Middle East. In Afghanistan, the Soviet army was getting beaten by the Afghan guerillas, with the help of rocket launchers sold by Israel to Egypt, then sold to Saudi Arabia and smuggled to Pakistan, thanks to Congressman Charlie Wilson.

People became aware things were shady in government when Colonel Oliver North was caught selling arms to Iran, and using the money for the Nicaraguan Contras.

AIDS awareness became a central topic as celebrities united to raise money for research. Among the celebrities born under this transit were Danica Patrick, Lady Gaga, and the Olsen twins.

# Uranus in Capricorn

A penetrating and serious mind may see though all the restrictions of Capricorn, and get past all the reservations and conservatism. Radical and innovative work may break old patterns, and a new vision for the future may be presented. Foresight, combined with a strong intuition may enable people to look outside the box, and see greater business opportunities. Spontaneity may not be too strong, but with proper planning it is possible to overthrow the corrupt old ways and establish new law and order.

**The United States established a new order with Uranus in Capricorn from 1820 to 1828.** The Monroe Doctrine asserted that the United States would not tolerate the interference of any European powers in the Western Hemisphere, essentially making the USA the dominant force on this side of the globe. Power structures began to change in the USA when new political forms took shape. Previously, Electoral College votes for President were given by state legislatures.

The election of 1824 was the first one in which the popular vote determined the allotment of Electoral votes. Andrew Jackson won the popular vote in 1824, but due to a bargain between Henry Clay and John Quincy Adams, it was Adams who was chosen as President. This spurred popular action by Jackson's followers to form "political machines" which would organize the voters for the next election. Popular figures born under this transit were Ulysses S. Grant, Stephen Foster, and Clara Barton, founder of the American Red Cross.

**A major arms build-up took place during the next Uranus in Capricorn transit from 1904 to 1912.** During the Russo-Japanese War, the behemoth Russian fleet was destroyed by the more efficient Japanese fleet. Theodore Roosevelt reaffirmed the role of the Monroe Doctrine by saying the United States could use "police" powers to intervene in Latin American nations. Major corporations such as the railroads and oil companies found themselves broken up by "trust busting" law suits. There was a threat of financial panic in 1907, but it was warded off by J.P. Morgan and his banking concern.

"Muckraker" newspaper writers exposed the abuses of major corporations, leading to major reforms and regulations. Leading public figures born at this time were Ronald Reagan, Rex Harrison, and Edward R. Murrow.

**A "New World Order" was proclaimed by President George H.W. Bush when Uranus was in Capricorn from 1988 to 1996.** After the Gulf War and the collapse of the Soviet Union, the United States was left as the leading world power. Conservative governments such as Margaret Thatcher's in Great Britain and Bush's in America were swept aside for more modern leaders.

However, the Presidency of Bill Clinton came under withering attacks by right-wing groups who were more interested in character assassination than policy debates. New business structures, such as Microsoft, rose up to new heights as the Internet became the new frontier for capitalism

**With Uranus conjunct Neptune in Capricorn, the public became enthralled with an imaginary world that was electronically maintained.** By the middle of the decade, millions of home computers would be sold, new websites would be set up, and communication by e-mail would become the new way of contacting people.

Among the celebrities born at this time were Jeffrey Earnhart, Daniel Radcliffe, and Kristen Stewart.

# Uranus in Aquarius

Success with science and original ideas are hallmarks of this transit. Uranus in its own sign brings extraordinary talent, great mental ability, and lots of ingenuity. It is a time for coming together with others in a very sociable manner. There is a lot of optimism about the future, and a desire to fight for a better world.

Humanitarian causes and mass movements are popular at this time, though intellect alone may not solve all of the world's problems. There may be a desire to embrace ideals rather than people.

**"Jacksonian Democracy" marked the period from 1828 to 1836, when Uranus was in Aquarius.** The election of Andrew Jackson to the Presidency saw the first "man of the people" take power. The six previous Presidents had come from the Patrician class, but Jackson had been born into poverty. In opening up his government to the people, Jackson established the Spoils System ("To the victor belong the spoils") which turned government offices over to political hacks whose only qualifications were that they voted for Jackson. It was a time when the common man became more influential in political matters, and this period marked the beginning of political conventions. However, Jackson was nearly crushed to death at his own inauguration when thousands of the "common man" invaded the White House to shake his hand.

At the same time in Great Britain, there was a reform movement to extend the vote, and slavery was finally eliminated in the British Empire. In France, reforms started to take place under the progressive king, Louis Philippe. Among the visionaries born at this time were Emily Dickinson, Madame Blavatsky, and Geronimo.

**The world saw major upheaval when Uranus was in Aquarius from 1912 to 1920.** It started off well with the election of Woodrow Wilson, who continued the progressive reforms started by his predecessors. However, a revolution broke out in Mexico, involving that country in a decade of strife, and nearly involving the USA in a war.

Then, World War I broke out in Europe, bringing violent conflicts to the old regimes of Europe. The worst hit was the Russian monarchy, which was overthrown in the violent Bolshevik revolution.

The Treaty of Versailles, which ended the war, brought major changes in the map of Europe, breaking up old empires and creating new national bodies. President Woodrow Wilson justified involvement in the great war by saying the United States was "keeping the world safe for Democracy." Significant figures born at this time included Richard Nixon, Gerald Ford, and Orson Welles.

**Uranus in Aquarius from 1996 to 2004 saw a major change in moral thinking with the impeachment scandal of President Bill Clinton.** Though acquitted by the Senate, Clinton had his reputation smeared by smarmy sexual activity, outlined in graphic detail by the Starr report.

Major attitude shifts toward the Gay community took place with the murder of Matthew Shepard, who was beaten, tortured, and left hanging on a fence. The brutality of the crime made people stop and think how they would react if one of their relatives was murdered in such a manner. The public revulsion spurred the passing of anti-hate crime legislation.

The fledgling internet was threatened by the Y2K bug, a poor programming procedure which had the potential to make older computers think that the year 2000 was the year 1900. Fortunately, reprogramming was accomplished in time to make the Y2K bug a non-event.

This transit saw the rise of Al-Qaeda and terrorist attacks against American personnel abroad, culminating in the attacks on the United States on September 11, 2001. This brought about the "War against Terror" leading to attacks on Afghanistan, and later a regime change in Iraq. President George W. Bush explained why the United States was attacked by Al-Qaeda by saying, "They hate us for our freedoms."

# Uranus in Pisces

It is still possible to be far-seeing but not have bright vision. Talents for medicine and developing cures may be found here. There is also danger of mass deception and intoxication. A spirit of enlightenment may develop, but watch out that it does not degenerate into fanaticism. Worries about conspiracies and corrupt institutions could prey upon the mind. Conspiracies may rise up to fight shadow conspiracies. The result may be that the cure is worse than the disease. A sense of faith may be stronger than any mental planning.

**Uranus in Pisces from 1836 to 1844 marked a period of economic collapse, brought about partly by the Specie Act of 1836.** This bill required that Federal land could only be purchased with gold coins. Land speculators drained the resources of local banks by demanding their accounts be settled with gold. The result was that thousands of small banks did not have enough gold reserves and had to close their doors.

Political change was brought when the story spread that President Martin Van Buren was living an "aristocratic" lifestyle, and the public voted for William Henry Harrison, whose campaign was heavy with songs and parades, but light on the issues. Unfortunately, Harrison died from pneumonia only a month after his inauguration, not having time to bring about change. Fanatical religious fervor developed with the growth of new churches such as the Mormons and the Millerites (later to become the Seventh-Day Adventists), who preached about the imminent end of the world. Some self-righteous figures born at this time included John D. Rockefeller, J.P. Morgan, and George Armstrong Custer.

**A better economic period was found from 1920-1927 when Uranus returned to Pisces.** "The Roaring Twenties" appeared to be a time of economic boom, with a larger share of the wealth going to the upper classes. However, the lower classes, particularly the farmers, were having a hard time making ends meet. A new breed of "nouveau riche" millionaires rose up, partly through illegal bootlegging and smuggling during Prohibition.

Also fundamentalist churches started growing, and their influence was best seen at the Scopes Monkey Trial in 1925, in which the state of Tennessee used the law to ban the theory of evolution. Fascist movements such as the Nazi party in Germany and the KKK in America also appeared to fight chimerical conspiracies supposedly organized by Communists and Jews. Noted figures born at this time included Betty White, John Glenn, and Henry Kissinger.

**From 2004 to 2011, Uranus in Pisces included a time when incompetence and deceptions by the government were exposed.** The disaster of Hurricane Katrina showed how ill-prepared FEMA was in handling a major disaster. Confidence in the government response plummeted when President Bush praised the incompetent FEMA director with the words, "Brownie, you're doing a heck of a job."

Major banking firms were putting their money in toxic investments, and mortgage firms were offering refinancing to homeowners with unreasonable rates. The result was an economic meltdown in 2008, bringing about the worst economic collapse since the Great Depression.

In politics, a new faction rose up called the Tea Party, which spread delusional stories about President Barack Obama, that he was born in Kenya, educated by Communists, and was secretly a Muslim. Further fantasies were spread by the right-wing media about "Obamacare death panels", the spread of Sharia law in America, and the building of a mosque on the former site of the World Trade Center.

# Chapter 5
# Uranus in the Houses

## First House

People with Uranus in the First House may be independent and eccentric characters. They might be unconventional thinkers, full of original ideas, scientific talent, and individualistic behavior.

There can be a desire for constant change, and a need for sudden action. Such persons could have extreme viewpoints, and there maybe a desire for companionship, but also a need to seek out different partners. Dynamic figures who had this aspect were Aleister Crowley, Alexander Graham Bell, and Nikola Tesla.

## Second House

Unsettled finances and impulsive buying are traits to watch out for with a Second House Uranus. There is a potential for making money through inventions or innovative ideas. Borrowing and lending to friends may be a feature with this placement.

The person may value money for the freedom it brings, but may have little attachment to possessions. There might be a tendency to gamble, or be involved in the changeable nature of business. The person could have an attitude of "Easy come, easy go" about money. Prosperous personalities with this placement were Liberace, Ringo Starr, and Sean Connery
.

## Third House

These persons may have intuitive minds, but there also might be abrupt changes of mind. This house position marks the freethinker, the scientific mind, and the academic success. There may be a desire to uncover the unknown, or involvement with revolutionary thought. Such a person might attract intellectual friends, but there is a danger of upheavals with siblings. Ideas may come so quickly that is may be hard to keep them all in order, and there is the possibility of miscommunication.

Highly intelligent persons with this aspect included Albert Einstein, Marlon Brando, and John Dean.

# Fourth House

An unconventional home life may mark these individuals. Their family may treat friends like members of the family, and they might have an open door policy welcoming all guests. They might have grown up with sudden changes in the household and much moving.

There may be a difficulty in settling down, and they could leave home early. Under such a transit, people might not settle in a home easily, and there could be a desire to travel.

Some peripatetic family men are Alan Alda, Ernest Hemingway, and David Bowie.

# Fifth House

Unusual creativity and radical artistic styles could be found here. Such people may not accept social manners and morals, and may be prone to sudden relationships, followed by sudden separations. Their children could be very gifted. They could have to deal with changeable fortunes.

This would be a good aspect for an entertainer, living life on the road and moving from one role to another. Some entertainers who had this aspect were Johnny Carson, Bob Dylan, and Elvis Presley.

# Sixth House

Free-spirited and inventive persons may be found with Uranus in this house. Such persons are better off not being employed by others, but just be their own boss so they could indulge their own unusual work habits.

People with Uranus in this house may be attracted to unusual healing methods or alternative medicine. They should also watch out for sudden illness. With this placement of Uranus, there may be ability and talent in mathematics and science Making friends at work and being sensitive to working conditions may be possible, but watch out for nervous behavior or environmental changes.

Among the unconventional workers who have Uranus in this house of work are Sidney Poitier, Jack Kerouac, and John Wayne Gacy.

27

## Seventh House

Unconventional partners or multiple marriages after sudden separations may mark the lives of those who have this Uranus aspect. The person could be an adventurer, and might be linked to unusual people. An extraordinary marriage could bring about resentment and there may be a threat of a scandal.

There could be a desire for more freedom in the marriage. Spouses may need to watch out for sudden mood swings and other changes in the marriage. Other types of partnerships,such as in business, could also be stressful.. Some figures with relationships that are out of the ordinary include those of Sigmund Freud, Richard Chamberlain, and Diane Keaton.

## Eighth House

Sudden legacies or an ability to rebound after losses may be beneficial to persons with this aspect. There may be an interest in death, archeology, and spiritualism. It is a good placement for someone interested in antiques and making sudden finds of lost treasures at flea markets.

Uranus could also mark a sudden death, an early death, or a death so extraordinary as to make headlines. A person with this aspect could live to a ripe old age, but it is likely the passing will be a noteworthy event, as significant as someone who passed on at a younger age. Among the celebrities who passed on early were Arthur Ashe, Guy de Maupassant, and Princess Diana.

## Ninth House

Unexpected journeys or accounts about fabulous locations may be the result of Uranus in this placement. If a traveler, the person may need to study about the destination of a journey. A person may have unconventional religious beliefs, and be very good at prayer and meditation. A student may depart from orthodox beliefs and study the teachings of other religions.

A person could be philosophical and have a utopian sense of vision. On the negative side there could be fanatical devotion to cult ideals. Visionary travelers with this aspect have included Jules Verne, F. Scott Fitzgerald, and Paul Gauguin.

# Tenth House

An inventive temperament and an unwillingness to submit to authority might prompt a person with this aspect to become his own boss. Uranus could signify the ability to persevere in spite of opposition, and to rise and fall and rise again.

There may be a danger of seeming overconfident and radical, and others might want to retaliate. Yet, the world may recognize the genius and talent of the person rather than just the foibles. A reputation for difficult and eccentric behavior might be the talk of gossip, but those who know the person will be impressed with the talents displayed.

Some rising and falling persons have included Muhammed Ali, William Blake, and William F. Buckley, Jr.

# Eleventh House

A person may end up being judged by the friends that are kept, and with Uranus here one's associates may have a profound influence on the person's life. One might be drawn to freethinking and radical persons, living out their Bohemian attitudes. One of the results is that a person could be pegged as part of the "in crowd", and possibly lose individual appeal.

There is a danger of unreliable friendships, unreasonable quarrels, and impulsive connections. However, the best friends to seek out are those who maintain humanitarian attitudes, scientific inquiry, and political awareness.

Some celebrities known for their connections are Buzz Aldrin, Jim Backus, and Harry Belafonte.

# Twelfth House

A search for spiritual identity and intuitive abilities may be the growth needed with Uranus in this house. The desire for personal transformation may be sparked by an inner strength, which may bring out hidden abilities. Even so-called "experts" may not be aware of the true talents such a person may have. There may be secret friends (or enemies) a person may not speak about, and some connections may be a surprise to others. A person with this aspect may be good at keeping secrets.

Among the personally driven personalities were Fred Astaire, Wilt Chamberlain, and John Denver.

# Chapter Six
# Uranus in Aspect

## Midheaven conjunct Uranus

This person may have a reputation as a free spirit, and may be seeking a career that is personally liberating.

Sudden changes in career are possible, but the person may have enough knowledge of technical innovation to make personal demands from any company. Such a person could achieve fame and rapid advancement with new and sometimes revolutionary ideas.

## Midheaven challenging Uranus

Sudden change could mean shocking change to some people. The drive to get ahead may bring about personal changes in mind and body, leading to tension and nervousness.

Difficulty with parents could cause a sudden move. There may be a major change in reputation and career difficulties. It could also mark a desire to break out of a boring career.

## Midheaven cooperating Uranus

Originality and innovation are the standards of this person's career goals. There may be a need for a flexible career where freedom of expression is possible. Such a person may be better off working alone, away from the corporate grind.

Although trying a new and different approach may be beneficial, one should watch out for restless dissatisfaction, and constant changes in attitude.

# Ascendant conjunct Uranus

This person may have a great desire for freedom, and consider personal relationships to be restraining. A strong sense of individualism may cause a restless feeling, making one seem impulsive. Non-conformity might be the way of life, though others might regard such a person as aloof, detached and impatient. A short attention span could be a drawback.

# Ascendant challenging Uranus

There could be extreme tension and restlessness, with a desire to break all the rules. Relationship and marriage problems could be evident with a difficulty in settling down. A person may want relationships but without stability and commitment. Friendship may be more important than romance. The biggest danger is the person could be so unstable, not even friends may be welcoming.

# Ascendant cooperating Uranus

There may be an appreciation of people with new ideas. The person may be seeking a sense of exhilaration, through new studies, new views and new adventures. Experiences and teachings may both be stimulating, as long as they are original.

A love of freedom will keep the individual from being caught in a routine or blindly following a crowd. The love for a group will come only when the group is doing something different.

# Sun conjunct Uranus

This is an aspect that can be considered as a sign of genius and inspiration. A person with this conjunction may have a restless need for originality, and a drive for creativity.

To others, such a person may seem eccentric and unpredictable. The desire for freedom might make this person hard to peg into a category. Bright talents may shine forth and bring radiance to the lives of others.

# Sun challenging Uranus

There is a danger of acting erratic and eccentric. A person could get a reputation for being unwise, irrational, and impractical. There could be an ego-connection with points of view, leading to impatience, hypersensitivity, and selfish behavior. This is the sort of person who might force change, even if it causes deep antagonism.

## Sun cooperating Uranus

This person may be creative and adventurous. Personal magnetism and a strong will could mark leadership ability, inspiring enthusiasm in others. A broad-minded humanitarian with a charismatic character, the person may attract others with original and unique perspectives.

Desires for liberation from set patterns may be the sense of freedom that others seek, bringing about a new movement of the masses.

## Moon conjunct Uranus

Emotional changes and impulsive behavior may be characteristics of this individual. The daily routine might be unusual and full of changes. People may be attracted to the artistic creativity, the freedom of expression, and the resourcefulness of this person.

This is a good aspect for a social leader, who may open up the home for meetings or gatherings of brilliant persons, such as a salon.

## Moon challenging Uranus

This person needs to watch out for unexpected emotional upheavals, sudden mood changes, and temper tantrums. Sometimes past trauma can lead to nervous tension and a desire to move frequently.

Constant changes of residences might prevent a person from putting down roots or even making steady friendships. With frequent separations and short-term acquaintances, the person may seem undependable and full of upset feelings.

## Moon cooperative Uranus

Taking chances with creative changes and developing new styles with radical innovation are signs of talent that this person may have. Although there may be rapid emotional responses, the person could have an unconventional sense of empathy, and may develop strong friendships with women. There may be a deep attachment to group activity. If such persons seem a bit odd, chances are their mothers are even odder.

## Mercury conjunct Uranus

New concepts come easily and are inspiring to this person. Open-minded attitudes and lively thoughts are positive signs of genius. Appreciation of a good education and an interest in science and electronics will inspire the individual, and mental work will take precedent over all other chores. There will be original and independent ideas flowing and inspiring others.

## Mercury challenging Uranus

A fast pace filled with hectic activity, and too many ideas coming at once may be a problem for this person. A constant need for stimulation may give annoying traits, eccentric opinions, and blunt speech. Nervous and impulsive behavior might make it difficult to reach a decision, and jumping to conclusions with inconsistent thoughts might alienate others. Intellectual conceit may prevent the person from taking advice, and there might be a reputation for being strange.

## Mercury cooperative Uranus

Brainstorming, scientific talent, and logical reasoning are powerful abilities for this person. Quick witted responses, inspiring thoughts, and dramatic attitudes are part of the individual appeal. Solutions to problems will come easily, especially with the help of a good memory. Apart from studies in technology, there might be advanced thought for Astrological studies. "Think for yourself" may be the motto of this person.

## Venus conjunct Uranus

Love at first sight, leading to intense affairs, could be a sign of this person who likes to take the initiative in romance. There is a need for an exciting relationship, with sparkling personalities, intense sociability, and even wild parties. Artistic talent may be found in this person, and the style may be very individualistic. The person could confuse friendship and love, and may quickly break off the relationship. There could be a desire not to be tied down, but also a desire to serve others, possibly multiple love partners.

## Venus challenging Uranus

The Seven-Year-Itch may arrive six years too early for this person, and there may be a restless desire for freedom, along with a wish to change lovers. The relationship may only be an infatuation, with little desire to accept responsibility. There may be a longing for a married person, or some other unusual partner, and concerns about divorce may not be a worry.

The aspect may also mean that the person could have an ambivalent attitude towards money and possessions, and that could mean spending on useless pleasures.

## Venus cooperative Uranus

Sudden love and intense excitement with a partner may be the emotional techniques of this person. This is a good aspect for someone in the arts and entertainment industries, and distinctive sex appeal could be the secret for popularity, bringing in numerous friends.

An unusual income source which is financially rewarding may be the main support and attract acquaintances with distinctive and fun-loving lifestyles. There may be respect for emotional freedom, and some spiritual involvement, but not too deep.

## Mars conjunct Uranus

Confrontational attitudes, a need for adventure, and desires for excitement and taking risks are found in this person. A strong fighter for social causes with a courageous demeanor and dramatic energy, this individual will not have a dull life. There might be an inclination to seek dangerous thrills or revolutionary activities. There may be some technical ability as well. This is a friend who will fight for you, and it would be better to have this person as a friend rather than as a dangerous and formidable enemy.

## Mars challenging Uranus

Reckless behavior, impatience, and angry confrontations are problems to watch out for. There may be too much assertive "In-your-face" attitudes, with explosive outbursts and quick-tempered attacks. Even anger expressed in an idealistic cause can seem erratic and immoderate. This person needs to beware of taking too many risks, craving too much excitement, and hurrying too much to the point of having accidents.

## Mars cooperative Uranus

Creative work, great expression, and unique accomplishments are virtues of this person. There may be a lot of hard work, filled with resourceful and energetic activity. Adventurous achievements and a forceful attitude may be coming from this person, with a strong willpower and a drive for decisive action. There is a need to seek out unusual experiences; otherwise a lot of nervous energy may be bottled up.

## Ceres conjunct Uranus

This person may have had a saintly mother who was there full-time lavishing love. The maternal influence may be manifested through humanitarian causes and wanting to heal others. Self-sacrifice and philanthropy may be traits of this individual.

Medical knowledge and even spiritual healing may be abilities developed for the care of all. Unique cooking talents and psychotherapy skills could bring comfort.

## Ceres challenging Uranus

Unstable nurturing as a child could cause a stressful life and difficulties in forming relationships. Fear of abandonment and a low self image might sabotage attempts at intimacy. Panic attacks and hysteria may bring a need for therapy.

Lack of self-worth might make friendships difficult, as other people would not be able to relate to the individual and find a common bond. A person might need counseling for self-development and creating a sense of personal value.

## Ceres cooperative Uranus

A positive sense of self-worth comes from self-love and personal development. This person may appreciate the good things in life, and is willing to share them with others. A fine meal, happy conversation, and emotional bonding could mark the loving reputation of a society leader. For such a leader, a political "party" could be a real party, with a good time had by all.

Promoting causes, planning fundraisers, and even making infomercials for the needy might be some of the talents of this big-hearted individual, inspiring others to follow a similar path.

## Jupiter conjunct Uranus

The blessings of sudden luck, abundant opportunities, and expansive breakthroughs are possible. There may be unusual advantages, help from friends, and unexpected sources of aid, such as education possibilities or travel experiences. The individual may have progressive thoughts, plans for original procedures, and talent for being a reformer or an advocate for a greater cause, along with a sense of generosity towards friends.

35

# Jupiter challenging Uranus

This person may not be too concerned about finances, and gambling losses or business risk-taking could lead to money problems. There could be difficulties with an unrealistic imagination, an undiplomatic personality, and a provocative nature which promises more than can be delivered. Such a person could be socially unpopular, with unreliable friends and a restless lifestyle that gives an urge for aimless travel.

There is also a danger of eccentric religious beliefs, leading to delusional and fanatical attitudes. A sense of over-confidence might make the person take a leap of faith, but then abandon the cause if things do not work out as imagined.

# Jupiter cooperative Uranus

Optimism, good feelings, and great insight may be positive traits for this individual. There may be a seeking out of a new philosophy to enhance the spiritual life. Profits may come from new advancements, creative ability, and an awareness of science.

Others may see the person as a leader for the qualities of philanthropy, altruism, and inspiring others. Unusual travel adventures, a desire to teach, and a need to be entertaining will increase social popularity.

# Saturn conjunct Uranus

Stability versus change are issues to be resolved by this person. There can be disciplined work, but a desire to change rigid concepts and come up with a practical expression of original ideas. There may be self-discipline, and a talent for mathematical and scientific study. In social settings, the person may seem abrupt, and there may be some suppressed tension. This is the sort of builder who could erect new structures on old foundations.

# Saturn challenging Uranus

Comfortable reality may be threatened, and there could be tensions with others. Even though the person can do disciplined creative work, there may be the experience of sudden career changes. A conflict between conservative and radical views may present a problem, and a resistance to innovation could cause the person to be swept away by change. The individual could be dictatorial, but still spout progressive views. Inconsistency and hypocrisy could lead to a downfall.

## Saturn cooperative Uranus

Blending the old and the new can bring in new ideas and release those which do not work. Original concepts can be applied in a practical way, and organizations can benefit from this person's scientific ability, genius for planning, and talent for finding constructive solutions.

Strong willpower, honesty, and a sense of loyal friendship are good virtues for statesmen, diplomats, or public relations people. Insights into the laws of nature and a skill for developing resources could make this individual all the more impressive.

## Neptune conjunct Uranus

This aspect took place in the 1990's, at the time when the Internet was developed for public use. People were immediately attracted to this imaginary world based on electronic constructs. It became seen as having a great potential for knowledge, scientific progress, and business expansion.

Unfortunately, the Internet has also gotten a reputation for deception, propaganda, and financial fraud. Nevertheless, the computer age has been regarded as a period of evolutionary development, and for the first time in history the younger generation is more educated than the older generation. The children born under this aspect have greater prospects for research, originality, and creativity.

## Neptune challenging Uranus

Danger of addiction, emotional turmoil, and nervous strain may be problems for a person with this aspect. Social unrest may lead to inharmonious conditions, and force persons to choose sides. Attitudes expressed by groups with insecure philosophies could be extremist and unreasonable.

The individual could be left with emotional confusion, highstrung turmoil, and nervous strain. These aspects were found in the early 1900's (when labor movements and women's suffrage rose up), the 1920's (during Prohibition and the rise of dictators) and the late 1950's (when civil rights workers and the Beat generation were expressing themselves.)

## Neptune cooperative Uranus

An expansion of consciousness, a visionary spiritual life, and New Age teachings are elements of this aspect. The person may be part of an idealistic generation, seeking to expand consciousness, promote artistic advancements, and join organizations that are part of a foresighted movement.

This aspect is found with the early Baby Boomer generation (with a post-World War II vision for world peace and a love for the suburbs), the 1960's New Frontier generation (with a love for space travel and scientific inquiry), and then the late 1970's generation (with a penchant for "Star Wars" and videogame entertainment possibilities.)

## Pluto conjunct Uranus

An aspect from the mid-1960's (taking place just as "The Munsters" and "The Addams Family" were filling the TV airwaves) this marked a time of radical change, new world views, and mass movements. The peace movement was marching along with the civil rights movement, and that sent fear though the outmoded social institutions that collective power would end their authority. Power was used for selfish purposes to repress movements, but the reforms demanded came to pass. Persons with this aspect may be described by two of the most powerful chants from the period, "Hell no, we won't go" and "We shall overcome."

## Pluto challenging Uranus

An aspect being felt at the time of this writing (and previously experienced during the Great Depression) we could be having a generational change, with drastic economic shifts and the mass destinies of nations played out.

New social programs may try to prevent insecurity, but economic problems may be too difficult for the solutions offered. Threats of war and violence could prompt people into joining fanatical and revolutionary groups. Decisions made at this time could set countries and organizations on a path to future upheaval, violence, and collapse.

## Pluto cooperative Uranus

This aspect was seen at the beginning of the Roaring Twenties, the end of World War II, and during the Internet boom of the 1990's. These were periods of major scientific change, sexual awakening, and the revealing of secrets. The most recent aspect saw the Clinton impeachment scandal, the death of Princess Diana, the revealing of Catholic sexual abuse scandals, and even congressional infidelity stories by Larry Flynt.

Persons born under this aspect may have a dynamic will, greater awareness of what is going on, and an inability to keep a secret. When cameras are everywhere, who can even try to keep things hidden?

# Eris conjunct Uranus

This aspect last took place in 1927, as both Eris and Uranus were entering Aries. Upheavals were starting to take place with new technology. Charles Lindbergh made his solo flight across the Atlantic, showing the world had become a smaller place.

The wealthy world of silent movie stars came crashing down with the coming of Talkies. Radio was being regulated, and the Columbia Broadcasting System set up the first network. Experiments were being made with television.

The next Eris-Uranus conjunction will be in 2016, and it is possible we will be seeing major technological upheavals by that date. At present, there is talk that Cable TV and the DVD may become as obsolete as silent movies, since people can download shows and music on the Internet. Universal Wi-Fi might do away with personal Internet connections. Smart Phones could develop more apps than ever imagined today.

# Eris challenging Uranus

Challenging aspects with Eris are not necessarily bad. Under previous challenging aspects, we saw the Vatican announce that the theory of evolution was worthy of study (1950), electronic music came into vogue (1964), the colorful Apollo 14 Moon mission took place (1971), the first test tube baby was born (1978), and the space shuttle program resumed after a six-year hiatus (1992). Scientific changes and a new opening up to greater world views are elements of these aspects. There may be more curiosity and stronger desires to solve problems in the persons with these aspects.

# Eris cooperative Uranus

The mythology of Eris is that she causes the most trouble when she pretends to be your friend. When Eris has been cooperative with Uranus, that is when major upheavals have taken place such as the Italian invasion of Ethiopia (1935), the Battle of Kursk (1943, the largest tank battle in history), the launching of Sputnik (1957, which sent fear and panic though the USA space program), the Hezbollah bombings and the sinking of the Greenpeace ship, the Rainbow Warrior (1985), the War on Terror (2001), and the banking collapse (2008).

Complacency may take a hit when these aspects come together, and the next one will be a semi-sextile in 2025. The consequences of events during these aspects are played out later, but at the time of the aspect there is a shock over the mass movement caused by a sudden event.

## North Node conjunct Uranus

There may be sudden changes, particularly sudden career moves caused by the new times. Spiritual values may be stimulated, and there could be great empathy for those suffering from the same issues. A desire for humanitarianism and philanthropic aid could be expressed.

## South Node conjunct Uranus

Personal upsets could be brought by the changing times. There may be fears over material losses. Traditional values may be challenged. There may be an inclination to hold on to what is on hand, and turn a blind eye to the suffering of others.

## North Node challenging Uranus

A person's values could be out of step with the latest mass movement going on. One might need an attitude adjustment or a reappraisal of the ethics system. There is also a possibility that a person may need to speak up to those who express disapproval, even if they outnumber the speaker.

## South Node challenging Uranus

Can a person afford to take a stand? The question may not be "What is right?" but rather "How much do I stand to lose?" There may be a willingness to go along with the majority, even if one sees that they are in the wrong. Weighing the decision could be a form of non-commitment in itself.

## North Node cooperative Uranus

There may be an ability to anticipate sudden changes. The person may be a good social reformer, capable of changing attitudes and capturing the public imagination. There could be a talent for being ahead of the curve, and foresee coming events.

## South Node cooperative Uranus

A person could be swept up by whatever popular movement comes along, and that could be a good thing. There may be a chance for personal advancement and networking. It could be a matter of "who you know" as opposed to "what you know."

# Chapter Seven
# Uranus aspecting Uranus

Since the 20th century, Uranus has replaced Saturn as the planet of old age, because people are living closer to the time of a Uranus return at age 84. Along the path of life, Uranus makes transits to its natal position, and these are usually found at specific ages in life.

## Uranus sextile Uranus
This aspect takes place at age 14 and age 70. In the teenage years, mental growth, group activities, and development of communication skills are vital for continued social growth.

Some of these elements can also be found around age 70, as new skills may be taken up to ward off mental inertia, group activities are indulged in, and communication skills get a work-out as new friends and acquaintances are made to fill in the gaps left by lost loved ones.

## Uranus square Uranus
Unreasonable, obstinate, and rebellious are the elements found in ages 21 and 63. The 21-year-old is seeking independence and a break from the domination of the family. At age 63, a person may be looking forward to leaving the working world and setting a new course in life. Youth may see a new career as a step forward in personal freedom, but by age 63 the attitude may be, "Take this job and shove it." The desire to be a free spirit might make both youth and old age seem cantankerous.

## Uranus trine Uranus
By age 28 a person may be settling in to a new career and prospects for the future. It may be a time of establishing an adult identity, though still taking chances and wanting to do as you please.

By age 56, "do as you please" may no longer be pleasing. The adult identity is firmly established, and career goals were accomplished. A person might start working on "the bucket list" deciding what needs to be done before passing on.

## Uranus opposing Uranus

The dreaded mid-life crisis hits around age 42. Is this all there is? Where is the romance in life? Sudden flings could lead to break up of marriages and relationships.

The need for sexual expression may be part of a desire for a change in style, and a new outlook on life in order to show that old age will not be here too soon. The danger is that desire for sudden change may alienate friends and lovers who are not used to the emotional up-heaval being expressed.

## Uranus Return

As scientific advances keep improving health, age 84 does not have to be the end of life, but it is a time to start thinking about legacies and what sort of reputation is left behind. As in infancy, there may be a need for the help of others, and one may seek out support groups and medical care.

The technical side of Uranus may be a benefit to some senior citizens who may be able to establish new social contacts thanks to the Internet and cell phones. One might come to see the value of George Bernard Shaw's statement that, "A life spent making mistakes is more useful than a life spent doing nothing."

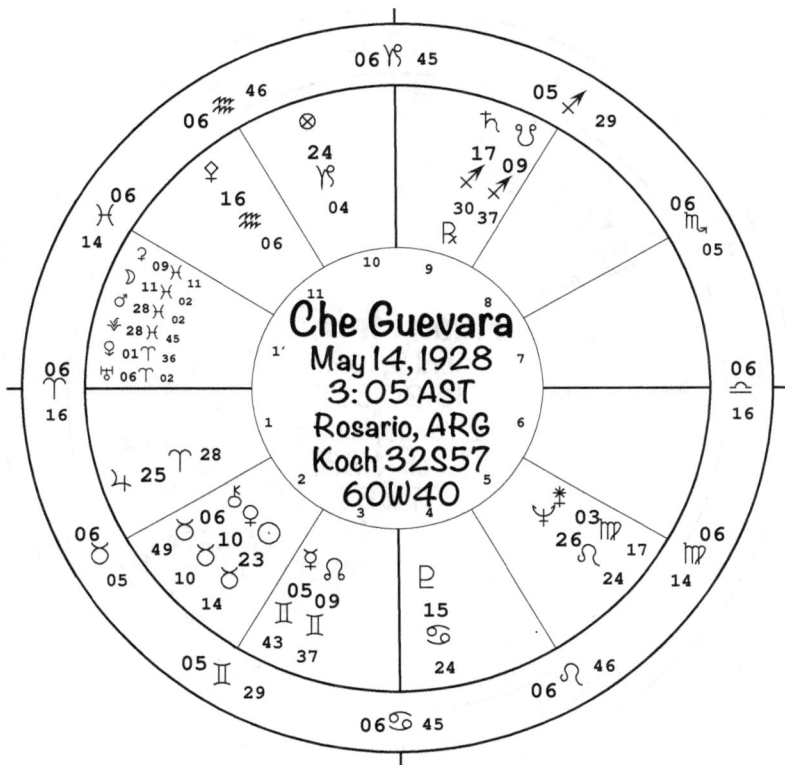

Che Guevara
May 14, 1928
3:05 AST
Rosario, ARG
Koch 32S57
60W40

With Uranus Rising, Che Guevara was considered the very model of a Marxist revolutionary. Natal Uranus was sextile Mercury, and he was very well educated as a medical student, becoming a doctor in June, 1953, when transiting Uranus was conjunct his Pluto.

His travels around South America showed him the inequities and cruelties of the political systems. When transiting Uranus was trine his Mars and square his Jupiter, he met Fidel Castro in Mexico City, and joined the cause of the Cuban revolution. His service during the revolution made him a national hero in Cuba.

During the 1960's, as Uranus transited through Virgo, he became a world traveler, spreading Marxist teachings from New York to Africa. While helping Bolivian guerillas in October, 1967, he was captured and executed at the time of the Uranus-Pluto conjunction.

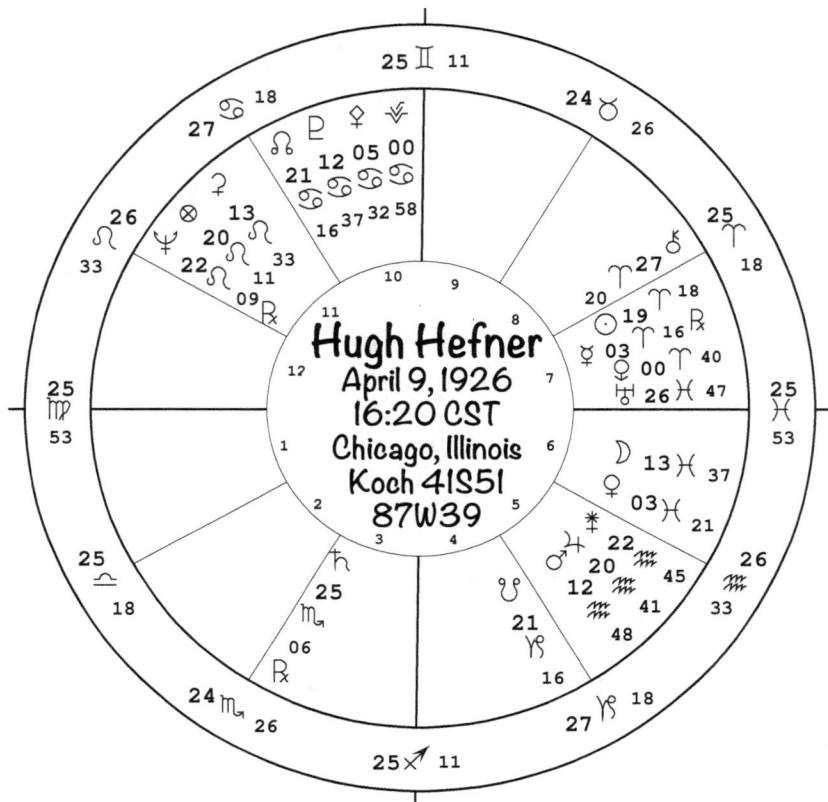

Hugh Hefner
April 9, 1926
16:20 CST
Chicago, Illinois
Koch 41S51
87W39

Although a successful magazine publisher and creator of the "Playboy philosophy," Hefner did not find long term marital happiness. With Uranus on the Descendant, conjunct Eris, he became a prominent figure, always surrounded by beautiful women and throwing lavish parties. His first marriage was in 1949, when transiting Uranus was conjunct his Vesta and trine his Venus. The marriage produced two children, but ended in 1959 (transiting Uranus conjunct Ceres) once Hefner promoted the hedonistic Playboy lifestyle.

Hefner did not marry again until age 63, when transiting Uranus was opposing his Vesta, and squaring his Eris. The marriage to Kimberley Conrad (age 27) produced two sons and only lasted nine years, but she ended up moving to the mansion next door to Hefner. Around the time of his Uranus return, Hefner met Crystal Harris, (age 23) and they were going to marry in June, 2011, but she called if off at the last minute. They finally did marry on Dec. 31, 2012, when transiting Uranus was conjunct his Mercury and Eris, and squaring his Vesta and Pallas.

44

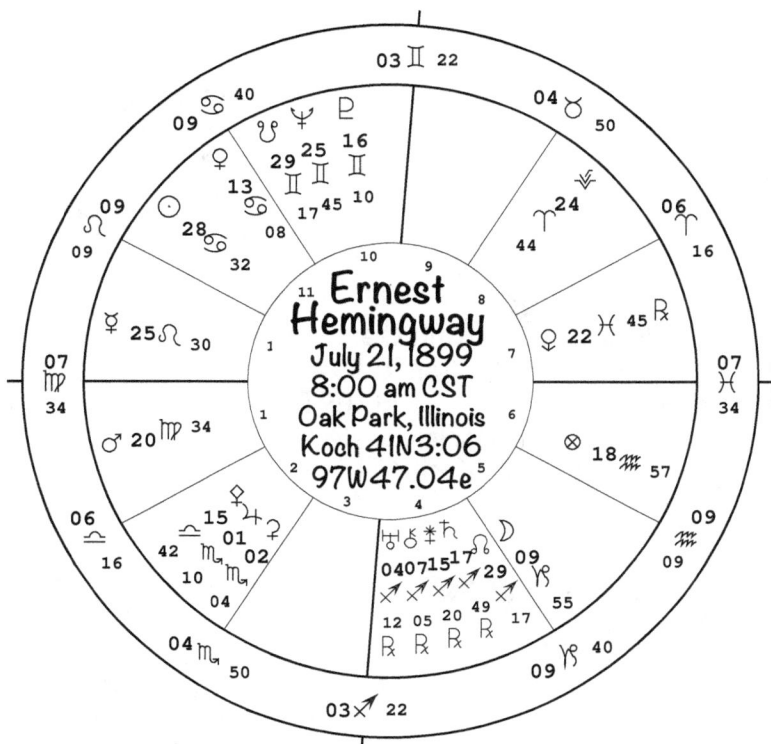

With Uranus on the IC, Hemingway had difficulties dealing with family life, perhaps emotionally scarred by a domineering mother, who kept him in "Buster Brown" clothes and curly hair until age 8 (transiting Uranus on natal Moon). His adult life of world travel, marlin fishing, lion hunting, and running with bulls may have been a lengthy protest against Mom.

Literary success began in 1926 (transiting Uranus trine Sun), with "The Sun Also Rises." With Uranus sextile his Venus in 1937, he covered the Spanish Civil War, and had a love affair with Martha Gellhorn, which gave him material for "For Whom the Bell Tolls," published with transiting Uranus square Mercury, and semi-sextile Neptune-Vesta. When Uranus was opposing natal Uranus, he was a correspondent in WWII, and nearly died from pneumonia. After the war (Uranus conjunct Pluto, then opposing Juno and Saturn), literary output declined due to crises and depression. Still, in 1952 (Uranus conjunct Venus), he won a Pulitzer Prize for "The Old Man and the Sea." In 1954, (Uranus conjunct Sun), two plane crashes nearly killed him, but he got the Nobel Prize for Literature. In 1961, (Uranus conjunct Mercury) he had a stroke, which left him mentally impaired and suffering from depression, which may have brought about his suicide on July 2.

45

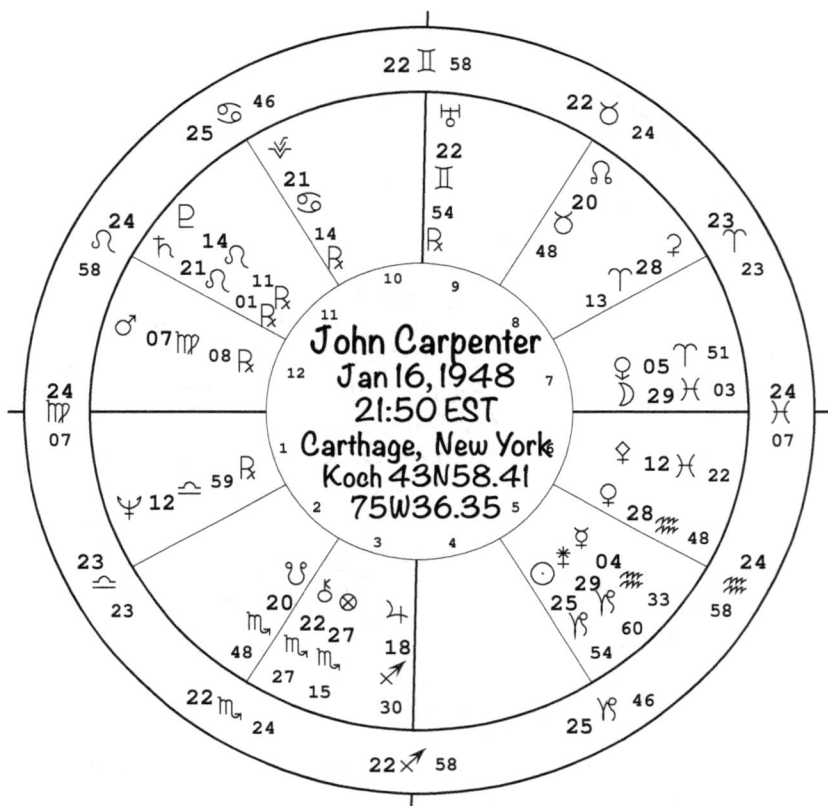

22 ♊ 58

25 ♋ 46

⚷ (figure)

21 ♋

22 ♊ 54 ℞

22 ♅ ♊

℞

22 ♉ 24

☊ ♉ 20

13 ♈ 28 ♃

23 ♈ 23

24 ♌ 58

℞ ♄ ♇ 14

21 ♌ ♌ 11 ℞ 01 ℞

14 ♋ ℞

10

11

9

8

♂ 07 ♍ 08 ℞

12

John Carpenter
Jan 16, 1948
21:50 EST
Carthage, New York
Koch 43N58.41
75W36.35

7

♀ 05 ♈ 51
☽ 29 ♓ 03

24 ♍ 07

1

24 ♓ 07

2

5

☿ 12 ♓ 22

♀ 28 ♒

♀ 48

♆ 12 ♎ 59 ℞

3

4

☉ ✷ ☿ 04 ♒
29 ♑ 33
25 ♑ 60
54

24 ♒ 58

23 ♎ 23

☊ ♐
20 ♏ ⊗
22 27
♏ ♏
27 ♏ 15

24 ♃
18
♐
30

25 ♑ 46

22 ♏ 24

25 ♑

22 ♐ 58

Uranus on the Midheaven helped this talented film director, who is credited with creating the genre of the "slasher" films. In 1978, when transiting Uranus was squaring his Pluto, Carpenter made the film "Halloween,"with a budget of $320,000. The movie made a profit of $65 million, and made its star Jamie Lee Curtis a leading "scream queen."

Transiting Uranus was square his Saturn in 1980 when he made "The Fog," which he considered to be a minor horror film. In 1981, transiting Uranus was trine his Moon, and he made the sci-fi classic, "Escape from New York," which made a $25 million profit.

During the years of Uranus in Sagittarius, Carpenter had several successes, but during the years of Uranus in Capricorn in the 1990's, Carpenter's films had less success. By the time Uranus entered Aquarius, Carpenter had gone into semi-retirement.

He was one of the first directors to promote video games, and that brought about business connections between films and the gaming industry.

# BIBLIOGRAPHY

Crowley, Aleister, *The Complete Astrological Writings*, edited by John Symonds and Kenneth Grant, Tandem Publishing Ltd., London, UK, 1976.

George, Llewellyn, *A to Z Horoscope Maker and Delineator*, Llewellyn Publications, St. Paul, MN, 1972

Moore, Marcia and Douglas, Mark, Astrology: *The Divine Science*, Arcane Publications, York Harbor, ME, 1978

Murphy, Simonne, *Ceres in Signs, Houses, Aspects*, ACS Publications, Epping, NH 2013

Negus, Joan, *The Book of Uranus*, ACS Publications, San Diego, CA, 1996

Sakoian, Frances & Acker, Louis, *The Astrologer's Handbook*, Harper & Row, New York, NY 1973

Simms, Maria, *Future Signs*, ACS Publications, San Diego, CA, 1996.

# INTERNET SOURCES

*When & Why did Uranus become associated with Aquarius*
*http://www.skyscript.co.uk/ur_aq.html*

*Uranus: The Discovery*
*http://en.wikipedia.org/wiki/Uranus*

*Uranus: The Mythology*
*http://en.wikipedia.org/wiki/Uranus_(mythology)*

# ABOUT the AUTHOR

Thomas Canfield, usually called Tom by his family, friends and colleagues, manages chart services for Astro Computing Services, our astrological chart and calculation service. Tom has studied astrology for many years, and with Virgo rising and Mercury in Capricorn, he works hard to keep facts and dates accurate. Since his Sun is in Aquarius, he was quick to volunteer to write our *All About Astrology* booklet for for Uranus, ruler of his sign, when we decided it was time to expanded the AAA booklet series by adding planets that didn't yet have their own booklet.

Previously, Tom wrote a quite interesting book about Eris. She was named for a goddess of discord simply because when first found beyond Pluto and larger than he, she upset what we knew about our solar system. Tom's book is *Yankee Doodle Discord,* subtitled *A Walk with Planet Eris through USA History*. All of us at ACS Publications were very pleased to publish it in 2010, and highly recommend that you read it, too! To make it easy to find where Eris is in your charts, the book has easy lookup tables of her zodiacal position for the years 1700-2050.

Tom also wrote our AAA booklet, *Eris in Signs, Houses and Aspects*. It's been interesting (and puzzling) to all of us why there still seems to be resistance to Eris among some who work with astrology—usually everyone is eager to try out a new planet! Well...here is Uranus, a planet that can be upsetting or exciting....and most often it's our choice that matters the most! Enjoy!

—Maria Kay Simms

# Hey, astrologers....are you including Eris as a planet in your charts?

Eris was discovered in 2006. She is a larger planet beyond Pluto, who was then named for a Goddess of Discord because her discovery had upset what we all thought was our known solar system.

After that, the astronomers decided to promote Ceres, the largest asteroid between Mars and Jupiter, to also be a planet. Then later, they decided that Pluto and all planets discovered beyond his orbit would be called "dwarf planets," a term that was later changed to "minor planet."

So, since 2006, children who are in grade school have had to learn about this, so it has been puzzling to us, here at Astro, that is now 2016 and still there are many astrologers who do not yet include or want Eris in their charts, are still using Ceres as just one of the four major asteroids...but virtually nobody has demoted Pluto.

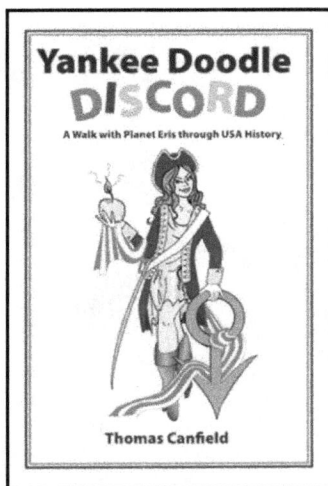

**Yankee Doodle DISCORD**

A Walk with Planet Eris through USA History

**Thomas Canfield**

$15.95

It's high time to include Eris and Ceres in your charts! Tom Canfield's book,shown above, will to help you learn about Eris and how she has worked in many charts of people significant in USA history and also in the charts of important events for which the time of inception is known. We've also published two of the booklets that are in our **All About Astrology** series, one by Tom on *Eris* and the other one was written by Simonne Murphy on *Ceres*.

Both of the booklets have interpretations for how these two new planets might work in the signs, houses and aspects.

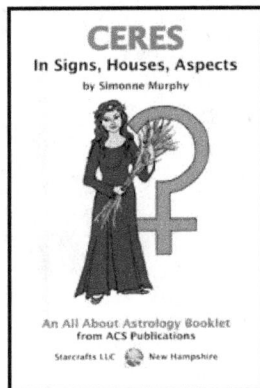

**CERES**
In Signs, Houses, Aspects
by Simonne Murphy

An All About Astrology Booklet
from ACS Publications

Starcrafts LLC ⬤ New Hampshire

$8.95

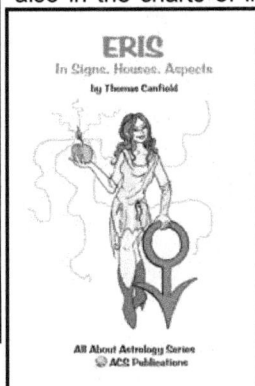

**ERIS**
In Signs, Houses, Aspects
by Thomas Canfield

All About Astrology Series
© ACS Publications

$8.95

Order book or booklets and many other useful books, charts, tools and calculations from Astro Computing Services!

**www.astrocom.com**

or call us Monday through Friday 603 734 4300
10 am to 3pm, Monday through Friday, Eastern Time.